The Adventures of Alfie and Pepper

Five Story Collection

By Siân Lewin
Illustrations by Alex Robins

Copyright © Siân Lewin 2021

ISBN: 978-1-9196151-4-1

Siân Lewin has asserted her right to be identified as the author of this Work in accordance with the Copyright, Designs and Patents Act 1988.

All rights reserved.

No part of this publication may be reproduced, stored in a retrieval system, or transmitted in any form or by any means, electronic, mechanical, photocopying, recording or otherwise, without the prior permission of the copyright owner.

Designed by Fuzzy Flamingo
www.fuzzyflamingo.co.uk

For all children and parents who love a story at the end of the day, especially about dogs, so enjoy Alfie and Pepper and snuggle down to sleep.

Contents

Alfie and Pepper Go to the Farm Park   1

Alfie and Pepper Meet the New Baby   15

Alfie and Pepper Go to the Seaside   27

Alfie and Pepper and the Christmas Tree   39

Alfie and Pepper Go on a Narrowboat   51

Alfie and Pepper Go to the Farm Park

Alfie and Pepper were fast asleep in their beds, when they heard the kitchen door open.

Alfie yawned and put his head under the blanket like always, whilst Pepper ran to the door. The only thing that would get Alfie out of bed was the sound of his biscuits being dropped into his bowl.

"Right, Alfie and Pepper," said their master. "Today we are going to the farm park. We are taking my godson, Charlie."

"Alfie, Alfie," barked Pepper to Alfie, "Wake up, we are going to the farm park with Master and his godson, Charlie!"

"What's a farm park?" barked Alfie.

"Well it's a farm and they have sheep, cows, hens, pigs and horses on show for people to look at," barked Pepper. "Lots of people live in cities and towns and don't get to see farm animals."

"That sounds like fun!" barked Alfie.

Master put Alfie and Pepper into the car and they drove off to the farm park, which was only a short distance away.

On the way, they picked Charlie up, who was very excited. It was his first visit to a farm park.

"Hi Alfie and Pepper!" He smiled at the dogs. Alfie especially was fond of Charlie, as he dropped treats when he was sitting having his food. "Uncle tells me we are having a picnic at the farm park, Alfie, so perhaps there might be a treat for you and Pepper!" Alfie was very hopeful when he heard this.

When they arrived, Master put Alfie and Pepper on their leads and they walked towards the animal pens.

In the first pen were some baby pigs. They were squealing and chasing each other around.

"Wow, they are fast!" barked Alfie. "Looks like they are having a great time."

"They are very cute," barked Pepper. "I'm sure they will be very sleepy soon."

In the next pen were some chickens, clucking and strutting about.

"Oh look," said Charlie, "they have laid some eggs. No wonder they are so happy."

The next pen had two very sleepy lambs in it. Their mother was lying next to them 'baaing' at everyone looking in.

"She looks very proud of her lambs," barked Pepper. "The mother is the sheep and the babies are the lambs, like dogs have puppies."

"I didn't know that, Pepper, you know everything!" barked Alfie.

They walked a bit further and came across a large field, which had some beautiful horses in it.

"Wow, they are big those horses," barked Alfie, "I am glad I am on the lead for once!"

At that moment, one of the horses bent over the rail and blew at Alfie!

Alfie jumped back and everyone laughed. "She was just saying hello, Alfie," barked Pepper. "I think she likes you!"

Master decided it was time to have their picnic, so they found a lovely spot under a tree, spread a blanket on the ground and got all the goodies out of the cool bag.

There were sandwiches, sausage rolls, crisps, apples, grapes and some rather delicious chocolate cake and, of course, some treats for Alfie and Pepper.

Charlie managed to sneak an extra treat to Alfie and Pepper, a bit of cheese sandwich. Alfie loved cheese!

After the picnic they tidied up, making sure that no litter was left anywhere.

"Alfie, it is so important to clear all your things up. That really was a nice picnic place," barked Pepper.

"Of course," barked Alfie. "I have eaten all my treats!"

The last part of the farm park was an area where you could hold some of the small animals.

There were rabbits and guinea pigs of all different colours.

Charlie was able to hold one of the rabbits, a black and white one, with a very twitchy nose. Alfie and Pepper were on the lead, of course, but looked on with interest.

Alfie had been told off once because he chased a rabbit. "I had just wanted to play with the rabbit!" barked Alfie.

"I know," barked Pepper, "but the rabbit was very scared as you were much bigger."

"They look so soft and Charlie is really enjoying holding it," barked Alfie. "This has been a great day seeing all the animals."

"Right," said Master, "I think it's time we went home. We will need to drop Charlie off first."

Once they had arrived home, Master gave Alfie and Pepper their dinner. They were both very tired after the excitement of the farm park.

"Which animal did you like best?" barked Pepper.

"I liked the piglets, they were funny when they were chasing each other around the pen. What did you like best?" barked Alfie.

"I liked the horses, they were so beautiful and it was funny when that one blew on you!" barked Pepper.

"It was really," barked Alfie. "Just made me jump a bit!"

Alfie and Pepper got into their beds and, before you could say fluffy rabbits, they were fast asleep.

Alfie and Pepper Meet the New Baby

Alfie and Pepper were fast asleep in their beds, when they heard the kitchen door open.

Alfie yawned and put his head under the blanket, whilst Pepper ran to the door. As always, Pepper was keen to get on with the day. The only thing that would get Alfie out of bed was the sound of biscuits and treats being dropped into his bowl.

"Right, Alfie and Pepper," said their master. "We have some visitors today and they are bringing their new baby."

"Alfie, Alfie," barked Pepper to Alfie. "We are going to meet a baby today!"

"Wow, a baby, is that like a puppy?" barked Alfie.

"Yes, that's right, it's a small new human," barked Pepper.

"That's exciting, I have never seen a baby before!" barked Alfie.

Master started to get the lunch ready, before the family arrived with the new baby.

Alfie and Pepper watched him, hoping that the odd bit might fall on the floor.

"Do you think we will get a treat if we are good with the baby?" barked Alfie.

"We should be good anyway, Alfie, without hoping to get a treat!" barked Pepper. "The treat is seeing the new baby!"

"That's not the same as a biscuit treat!" moped Alfie.

"You will love seeing the baby, Alfie, it's Master's grandson William and it's the first time he will have seen him," barked Pepper.

"All right I will be good," barked Alfie, "I'll try not to think about biscuits and treats, as I guess this is Master's treat."

A few minutes later, the doorbell rang and Master went to the door to let them in.

"Hi!" said Master. "Come in, Alfie and Pepper are very excited to see you all too."

"I'm a little nervous!" barked Alfie. "The bed the baby is in looks very small!"

"You'll be fine," barked Pepper. "Just wait until Master gives us the nod and we can have a look at the baby."

Master held the baby very carefully and gave the nod to Alfie and Pepper to come forward.

Alfie and Pepper moved forward slowly; they were both a bit nervous. Master moved the blanket back and both dogs peered in.

"Gosh, isn't he pink and small!" barked Alfie.

"His eyes are opening!" barked Pepper.

Master smiled. "This is my grandson, William. Alfie and Pepper, shall we take the baby for a walk before lunch?"

"Can the baby walk?" barked Alfie.

"No, of course not!" barked Pepper. "Human babies can't walk until they are nearly a year old, unlike puppies who can walk in a few days."

"Right!" said Master. "Let's put William in his pram and we can take him for a walk."

Alfie and Pepper walked proudly by the pram as they went down the road.

They saw their old friend Oscar ahead, who was a Welsh Border Collie.

"Hi Oscar!" barked Pepper. "We've got Master's new grandson William here in the pram, he's a baby."

"Oh, that's nice," barked Oscar. "Always fun when a new human joins the family."

"William is fast asleep," barked Alfie. "Pepper said I might get a treat if I am good!"

"Well, the treat is having the baby coming to see you!" barked Oscar.

"I guess so," barked Alfie, "but a treat would be nice."

Once they arrived home, Master said the baby needed changing.

"Changing!" barked Alfie. "Are we getting another baby?"

"No!" barked Pepper. "Babies have to wear a nappy to keep them clean and it now needs changing."

"Ooh, that's a bit smelly!" barked Alfie, twitching his nose.

"He will soon be all nice and clean," barked Pepper.

"Oh that's good," barked Alfie.

Master then showed Alfie and Pepper William all nice and clean.

"Alfie and Pepper, you have been so good I think a little treat is deserved," said Master.

"Yes!" barked Alfie. "But it has been a treat seeing baby William!"

Later that day, Alfie and Pepper got into their beds to go to sleep.

"What was your favourite bit of the day, Alfie?" barked Pepper.

"I think walking by the pram. I felt like I was guarding baby William!" barked Alfie. "I didn't like the changing of the nappy, it made my nose twitch!"

"It was a lovely day welcoming baby William," barked Pepper. "So nice to have a new little person in the family."

Master came in to say goodnight.

"Well done, Alfie and Pepper, here's an extra special treat for being so good with baby William."

Alfie and Pepper snuggled down in their beds with a lovely warm feeling and went fast asleep.

Alfie and Pepper Go to the Seaside

Alfie and Pepper were fast asleep in their beds, when they heard the kitchen door open.

Alfie yawned and put his head under the blanket, whilst Pepper ran to the door. As always, Pepper was keen to get on with the day. The only thing that would get Alfie out of bed was the sound of biscuits and treats being dropped into his bowl.

"Right, Alfie and Pepper," said their master, "we are going to the seaside today!"

"Alfie, Alfie," barked Pepper to Alfie, "we are going to the seaside today!"

"Wow, do we get to swim?" barked Alfie.

"Of course, Alfie, let's hope the water isn't too cold!" barked Pepper.

"If I dip my paw in the sea, that will tell me how cold it is," barked Alfie.

Master then put Alfie and Pepper into the car and they set off to the seaside.

"So remind me again," barked Alfie, "will we have biscuits and treats at the seaside?"

"You only think of biscuits and treats!" barked Pepper. "I am sure Master will make sure we have a little seaside treat!"

A while later, the car pulled up near the beach. Alfie and Pepper's heads popped up at the window. They had both had a nap whilst Master had driven the car.

Master let Alfie and Pepper out of the car, very carefully, in case there were other cars about.

He took them onto the beach and let them off their leads.

"I am excited!" barked Alfie.

"I am too!" barked Pepper.

They looked around the beach and there were several other dogs. Some were chasing balls and a little poodle was testing the water with her paw. She jumped back as the waves rushed in.

Alfie and Pepper ran down to the water's edge next to the poodle.

"Is it cold?" barked Alfie.

"It's a little chilly, but I think it will be all right," barked the poodle whose name was Lily.

Alfie gingerly dipped his paw into the water, just as a large wave came in and sent him toppling over.

"Alfie, Alfie, are you all right?" barked Pepper.

Alfie shook his head and body and barked, "Yes, but that wave took me by suprise!"

"That's why it's so important to learn to swim," barked Lily. "I learnt to swim when I was a puppy."

"I can swim too!" barked Pepper.

At that point, Master came over and said, "Right, Alfie, as you haven't been to the beach before, let's have a little swimming lesson. You have to be careful, as the sea is very strong.

Slowly, Master helped Alfie into the sea and he managed to swim a few doggy paddle movements. He felt much more confident in the water and it wasn't that cold.

"Well done, Alfie!" barked Pepper. "You will feel safer now you can swim."

"That's great!" barked Lily. "I'm so pleased to have met you both and so pleased to see Alfie learning to swim. It's so important for everyone to learn to swim, whether you are a dog or a human!"

Master called Alfie and Pepper over and shared some of his ice cream with them as a special treat.

"That was fun!" barked Alfie. "I felt very brave going into that big water."

"You were," barked Pepper. "I am very proud of you!"

"Let's get home now, Alfie and Pepper," said Master. "Well done again, Alfie, you were very brave!"

"Bye, Lily!" barked Pepper. "Have a safe trip home!"

"And you and Alfie," barked Lily.

Once they were home, Master gave them their dinner. Alfie was almost too tired to eat, with all the excitement of the seaside and learning to swim.

"Come on, Alfie," barked Pepper. "I think we need an early night, with all that fresh air and you learning to swim!"

"Yes, I am a little tired," barked Alfie. "I was very brave and feeling really proud learning to swim. The ice cream was nice afterwards too!"

"You always think of your stomach, Alfie," barked Pepper. "You'll never change; thinking of treats and biscuits will get you through anything."

Alfie and Pepper got into their beds to go to sleep and, before you could say biscuits, Alfie was fast asleep.

Pepper smiled to herself. She loved her friend Alfie and it had been such a lovely day.

Alfie and Pepper and the Christmas Tree

Alfie and Pepper were fast asleep in their beds, when they heard the kitchen door open.

Alfie yawned and put his head under the blanket like always, whilst Pepper ran to the door. The only thing that would get Alfie out of his bed was the sound of his biscuits being dropped into his bowl.

"Right, Alfie and Pepper," said their master. "Today we are going to get the Christmas tree ready for tomorrow."

"Alfie, Alfie," barked Pepper to Alfie. "We are going to get a Christmas tree!"

"What's a Christmas tree?" barked Alfie. "Is it a tree that we can eat?"

"No, Alfie, we don't eat it!" barked Pepper. "A Christmas tree is a pine tree, usually, that is brought into the house and decorated with lights, ornaments and whatever you want to put on it."

"Wow, that sounds exciting, I can't wait to see all the trees and run around looking for the right one!" barked Alfie.

Master put Alfie and Pepper into the car and they drove off to the garden centre to buy a tree.

"Goodness me!" barked Alfie once they had arrived. "There are so many trees here, I wonder which one we will have?"

Master chose a really bushy, bright green tree that was very tall. Alfie and Pepper were very excited and couldn't wait to get it home.

As they turned back towards the car, they bumped into Barney, their neighbour's Labrador.

"Hi Barney!" barked Pepper. "Are you here to get a Christmas tree too?"

"Yes!" barked Barney. "I'm here with my owner's son, as she is still resting after being in hospital."

"I hope she gets better soon," barked Alfie, "we've missed seeing you on our walks."

"Yes, her son takes me in a different field, so that's why I haven't seen you." barked Barney.

"Well, I hope she is soon out and about and walking you in our field!" barked Pepper. "We have missed seeing you, Barney."

Once they arrived home, the tree was put in a very large pot. Master then started to decorate it with lots of baubles, lights and a star on the top of the Christmas tree.

Alfie and Pepper watched closely and tried very hard not to play with the baubles when Master dropped them.

"They are a bit like the balls we play with in the garden!" barked Alfie.

"Well, you mustn't try and bite them, as they are very delicate and break very easily," barked Pepper. "The Christmas tree looks very beautiful and so colourful, even more when the gifts are under it!"

"Oh, it does. When do the gifts go under the tree, Pepper?" barked Alfie.

"Well, Father Christmas has to check his lists, to make sure everyone has been very good all year!" barked Pepper. "Being good isn't just for Christmas, Alfie, we need to try to be good every day."

"I have been good, most of the time," barked Alfie. "I do try, just sometimes I forget, so I hope I am on the good list."

The next morning was Christmas Day and when Master came to wake Alfie and Pepper up, they were both out of their beds, ready for the special day.

"Is there something for me?" barked Alfie. "I really have been a good dog and I even got out of bed early this morning, without a treat to tempt me!"

Master looked under the Christmas tree and pulled out two brightly coloured packages.

"Right, this one is for you, Pepper, as you have been very good!" said Master.

Alfie held his breath and waited; paws crossed he was on the good list.

"This one is for you, Alfie, for being good most of the time!" said Master.

Alfie and Pepper ripped open their packages and inside were lots of treats and gifts.

Alfie couldn't believe his eyes! First a yellow rubber chicken, with a very loud squeak, then a red ball and lots of Christmas-shaped dog biscuits.

Alfie loved the toys and wasn't sure which one to play with first.

Pepper had a beautiful new collar and an orange frisbee, her favourite toy, she loved to run fast.

"What lovely presents, I can't wait to play with my frisbee and wear my new collar," barked Pepper.

"I love my yellow chicken, it has the best squeak! This has been the best day ever, so many treats!" barked Alfie.

Later that day, Alfie and Pepper got into their beds, very tired after such a fun-packed day.

Master came in and gave them a big hug each. "Goodnight, Alfie and Pepper, what a lovely day it has been. We will have a lovely walk tomorrow and take your new toys!" said Master.

Before you could say happy Christmas Alfie and Pepper, both dogs were fast asleep; it had been a very exciting day.

Alfie and Pepper Go on the Narrowboat

Alfie and Pepper were fast asleep in their beds when they heard the kitchen door open.

Alfie yawned and put his head under the blanket like always, whilst Pepper ran to the door. The only thing that would get Alfie out of bed was the sound of his biscuits being dropped in his bowl.

"Right, Alfie and Pepper," said their master. "Today we are going on a holiday for a few days. We are going on a narrowboat!"

"What's a narrowboat?" barked Alfie to Pepper.

"A narrowboat usually goes on a canal, sometimes for a holiday and also for carrying goods to people living on the canal," barked Pepper. "We will have a fun time, Alfie, there's so much to see on the canal!"

Master packed the car up and they set off towards the canal, which was a short drive away from their home.

They all got out of the car, Master making sure both dogs were on the lead. They walked towards the marina, where all the narrowboats were kept. Master picked up the the keys and they headed towards the boats.

They found their boat, which was a bright blue colour with lots of flowers painted on it. The name on the side was Bluebell.

"All the boats are given a name," barked Pepper. "I guess ours is because of its colour."

"Let's put your life jackets on, Alfie and Pepper," said Master.

"What's a life jacket?" barked Alfie.

"Well, although you can swim, Alfie, there are some dangerous areas on a canal if you fall in and you might get pulled away from the boat," barked Pepper. "A life jacket helps you float in the water."

Alfie liked his shiny red life jacket. He felt very important and, most of all, safe.

Master moved the narrowboat onto the main canal and they started their adventure.

Alfie and Pepper looked onto the water and saw lots of ducklings with their parents, all paddling through the water as the narrowboat floated by.

"Oh look, Alfie," barked Pepper, "there is a swan with her cygnets. Aren't they lovely?"

Alfie was transfixed, looking at an animal that was sitting calmly on the side of the canal.

"That's a water vole," barked Pepper. "Look at him cleaning his whiskers."

The narrowboat then started to approach the locks and Master shouted to some people on the towpath to see if they could help.

"What is a lock?" barked Alfie.

"Well, it's one part of the canal blocked off by another. There are strong gates at either end. Water is pumped in and out, so we can move up to a higher or lower level of the canal!" barked Pepper, who, as always, knew everything.

"Wow, that is clever!" barked Alfie. "Will we be quite safe?"

"Yes, Master knows what he is doing and those people on the towpath are going to help him," barked Pepper.

Alfie and Pepper sat very still, both with their life jackets on, whilst the narrowboat went into the lock.

The water flowed into the lock and the narrowboat started to rise.

Once it had reached the top line, it stopped. Then the gates at the other end opened and the narrowboat moved forward through the gate and on with their journey.

"Well, that was exciting!" barked Pepper.

"It was. I'm glad I had my life jacket on!" barked Alfie. "I was glad when we got safely through."

As they went further down the canal, Master announced that they were going to stop for some lunch.

A brightly coloured pub was on the side of the canal. It had lots of tables with umbrellas up. Master chose a table near the water.

Lunch arrived for Master with a couple of extra bowls of rather tasty sausages for Alfie and Pepper.

"There is so much to see and do on the canal," barked Pepper. "These sausages are particularly delicious!"

"They are so tasty, what a special treat!" barked Alfie. "This is the best holiday ever."

Some children were playing next to them with a small puppy; a little furry bundle.

"Oh, isn't she cute?" barked Pepper. "I wonder what her name is?"

"My name is Lottie!" yelped the puppy.

"Hi Lottie, this is Alfie and I am Pepper," barked Pepper. "We are on holiday and having a wonderful time on the canal, staying on Bluebell, our beautiful narrowboat over there."

"I live here at the pub," yelped Lottie. "I have met so many new friends. It's lovely to meet you and Alfie."

Master then said it was time to get back on the narrowboat, so the dogs said goodbye to their new friend Lottie.

Once back on the narrowboat, Alfie and Pepper sat watching the canal, looking for more animals that lived on and by it.

There were a couple of people fishing on the bank. One of the fishermen waved at the dogs. Alfie and Pepper loved being waved at and wagged their tails in response.

A large bird landed on the side of a nearby boat. It was a heron with a huge beak.

"That is a very big bird," barked Alfie. "Do you think it's looking for treats?"

"More like some fish for its supper," barked Pepper.

The heron flew off, much to Alfie's relief; he was worried it might eat his treats, even though Pepper said it only ate fish!

A little while later, Master pulled Bluebell over to the side and moored up for the night.

"Well, this has been a lovely day," barked Pepper. "The canal is such a fun place. It was nice to meet Lottie too!"

The dogs got into their beds and, before you could say 'ahoy there', both dogs were fast asleep.

Meet the Real Alfie and Pepper

Alfie and Pepper are based on Siân's real-life pets.

Acknowledgements

Jen Parker – Editor and Designer

I was introduced to Jen a couple of years by a mutual friend and it was a great introduction! Jen has brought Alfie and Pepper further to life with her design, introducing the website on the back of the book and making the ISBN number look attractive. She  works hard to make your books the best they can be and her own drive and determination has resulted in her writing her own books. Jen is a delight to work with, her family are the centre of her world and her editing and design business Fuzzy Flamingo is a big part of her life as well. Many thanks to Jen for her support, dedication and most of all cheerfulness.

Alex Robins – Illustrator

My introduction to Alex was through my village Facebook, page after I posted an advert asking for an illustrator and received five responses, of which Alex was the first

 to respond. As it was during lockdown, we met online and chatted about the stories. I sent lots of photos of Alfie and Pepper and he came back with some sketches. Within a short time he got the essence and style of the dogs, especially Alfie who was a Border/Cairn Cross Terrier.

Alex's beautiful illustrations have brought Alfie and Pepper to life in the stories and he has done an extraordinary job.

Website

Through Alfie and Peppers website I have added audio and video, which I have narrated, telling the stories through the dogs' voices and mine, giving them their further identities. Alfie is the cheeky chappie and wants to find out so much more about life. He loves his treats and hopes that if he is a good boy he will be rewarded. Pepper is a Welsh Border Collie, very caring and likes to teach Alfie about life; she knows so much and Alfie is amazed by her knowledge. Each story has a little life lesson, mainly for Alfie. The stories start in bed with the dogs and then end in bed after their little adventure. I want children to see, that being in bed at the end of the day is the best place to be.

Check out Alfie and Peppers website for more information: www.theadventuresofalfieandpepper.com

Sian Lewin – The Author

Alfie and Pepper were the most wonderful dogs, full of fun and very much a part of the family. I wrote the first story when I was recovering from Hairy Cell Leukaemia in 2012, but put it in a drawer until 2021 when I had to shield. I wrote and recorded a further 8 stories about Alfie and Pepper. I originally trained to be an actor and recording the stories gave me a focus during lockdown.

Alfie and Pepper are calming stories for children, at the end of a busy day, it's lovely to snuggle down and have a warm and caring story read, whilst they fall asleep.

www.ingramcontent.com/pod-product-compliance
Lightning Source LLC
Chambersburg PA
CBHW041801290426
43661CB00133B/1277